They Knew Then

Character, Love, Money, Leadership,
And other sage advice,
3000BC – 1500 AD.

James Schaffer

authorHOUSE®

AuthorHouse™
1663 Liberty Drive
Bloomington, IN 47403
www.authorhouse.com
Phone: 1-800-839-8640

First published by AuthorHouse 8/31/2009

ISBN: 978-1-4389-7798-0 (sc)

Printed in the United States of America
Bloomington, Indiana

This book is printed on acid-free paper.

In fact, nothing is said that has not been said before.

-   Terence

-    190 – 159 BC

To my family,

Table of Contents

Preface

"If I knew now what I knew then," my father used to say. To that question I would always ask, "What would you do?"

Sometimes, it seems, days last for an eternity, and the past exists in the blink of an eye. But that past, our ancestral human past, has existed for almost 7,000 years, since our days in Mesopotamia. 7,000 years of human evolution, it's almost too much to comprehend. In fact, of those 7000 years, it's only been within the last 200 years that we could drive a car, fly a plane, or more recent still, chat on the internet.

In our recent/memorable world, we have made exponential strides in how we get around, in how we communicate, in where we live, in the food we eat et cetera; and given all this, when we think back to our ancestors thousands of years ago, it seems like they are merely pieces of fiction, found in religious texts or on movie screens. I think it is fair to argue that if we were to switch places with them, both of us would think we were lost on an alien planet, which would only serve our "fictional" perspective. Everything you would see, hear, touch and smell, would be as foreign as you can imagine.

Yet, given all these changes in our environment, given all the changes external to us, is there anything, any idea, any sentiment, that connects all people, present, and presumably, future? Is there anything of "universal value" that truly transcends time, transcends objects, that transcends culture? If so, what is it? What does that tell us about ourselves; about the human condition; about our own modernity?

Today we can fly to the moon, drive cars over 100mph, and trade with all corners of the globe, however, don't we want our mothers to care for our children? Do we want our father to be able to afford shelter and food? Do we want our friends and neighbors to act honorably and fairly? These values haven't changed in over 7,000 years. These are the questions and challenges that we continue to strive to solve. This is the human experience.

I chose to limit the time period from 1500 AD and prior for two, less than scientific, reasons. First, is the Charles Gutenberg printing press of 1436 AD. The printing press is generally considered as one of the most important inventions of our time. For the first time ever, knowledge was widely available and could be reproduced with great ease.

The second is William Shakespeare, born 1564. Shakespeare is widely regarded as the greatest writer in the English world, if not, the entire world. Shakespeare's mastery of language, dramatics, characters, and plot, forever changed and shaped our spoken and written word.

Given the dramatic influence these two men had on the accumulation of words and their usage, I wanted to capture the points of our history, before these paradigm shifts occurred. I wanted the pages which held these words to have withstood a physical and political 'survival of the fittest' test.

All authors and years are to the best of my knowledge accurate, though in some cases, there is still dispute regarding exact dates and authors. Also, most notably missing are ancient Mesoamerican writings, however, following the Spanish conquests, finding reliable sources is difficult. In future editions, I plan to remedy this omission.

I have also done my best to divide the quotes into the most relevant chapter headings.

Character – Explore what it is that makes us better men and women to our world.

Golden Rule – Examines the one moral principle that has stretched throughout all cultures; for all time.

Leadership – Regardless if you are a general on the battlefield or in business, leading men and women has the same rules.

Love – Covering everything from Men, Women, Sex and relationships

Money – That which makes the world go round.

Quips, quotes and other sage advice – Just a bit of perspective and a little insight into our world.

So we move toward our own future, looking for "the answers," whatever that may be, so maybe, a group of people who lived for a few thousand years before us know something, maybe, They Knew Then.....

A VERY Brief History of
Human Civilization...

200,000 BC – Homo Sapiens

70,000 BC – "Out of Africa" migration

5,000 BC - First Civilization – Mesopotamia

4,000 BC – Writing emerges (vs. drawings and illustration)

3000 BC – First Dynasty of Egypt

2630 BC –First Pyramid of Egypt (Djoser)

1800 BC – Birth of Abraham

1500 BC – Shang Dynasty (First Chinese Dynasty)

1300 BC – King Tutankhamen

1100 BC – Trojan War (1194–1184 BC)

800BC – First Alphabet (Greece)

500BC – Confucius (551 BC – 479 BC), 500 BC - Siddhãrtha Gautama (563 BCE to 483 BCE), Beginning of Greek Period

300 BC – Alexander the Great (356 BC – 323 BC)

350 BC – Plato (428/427 BC– 348/347 BC)

100 BC – Julius Caesar (July 13, 100 BC – March 15, 44 BC)

1-   Jesus Christ

300 AD – Peak of Mayan Empire

400AD – Begin the Fall of the Roman Empire

1000 AD – Age of Vikings

1041 AD – Bi Sheng invents a ceramic Moveable Type in China

1100 AD - Genghis Khan (1162)

1400 AD– Completion of Forbidden City in China, Joan of Ark

1436 AD - Johannes Gutenberg invents modern printing press

1500AD – Shakespeare 1564 – 23 April 1616

1512 AD – Copernicus places Sun in the middle of the Solar System

1776 AD – Declaration of Independence (US)

1800 AD – First Locomotive (Richard Trevithick)

1884 AD – First Car (Karl Benz)

1903 AD – First Aircraft (Wright Brothers)

1941 AD – First Computer (Konrad Zuse)

1969 AD – Man landed on the moon

1983 AD – First TCP/IP WAN operated

2009 AD – *They Knew Then*, published!

Character

Character is that which reveals moral purpose, exposing the class of things a man chooses or avoids.

- Aristotle
- 322 BC

Our discussion is about no ordinary matter, but on the right way to conduct our lives.

- Plato
- 428 BC – 347 BC

A superior man in dealing with the world is not for anything or against anything. He follows righteousness as the standard.

- Confucius
- 551 BC - 479 BC

Any can hold the helm when the sea is calm.

- Publlius
- 503 BC

One must steer, not talk.

- - Seneca
- - 54 BC- ca. 39 AD

There is nothing, absolutely nothing, which needs to be more carefully guarded against than that one man should be allowed to become more powerful that the people.

- - Demosthenes
- - 384–322 BC

The reason why we have to ears and only one mouth is tht we may listen the more and talk the less.

- - Zeno
- - 490–c.430 BC

Think before you act.

- - Pythagoras
- - 572 BC- 590 BC

What you do not want done to yourself, do not do to others.

- - Confucius
- - 551 BC - 479 BC

Let nothing be done in your life which will cause you fear if it becomes known to your neighbor.

- - Epicurus
- - 341 BC– 270 BCE

Patience is the best remedy for every trouble.

- Plautus
- 254–184 BC

First say to yourself what you would be; and then do what you have to do.

- Epictetus
- 55–ca. 135

You should not boast; then your words will be trusted.

- Instructions of Shuruppak
- 2600 BC

The universe is change; our life is what our thoughts make it.

- Marcus Aurelius
- April 26, 121– March 17, 180

Death hangs over thee. While thou still live, while thou may, do good.

- Marcus Aurelius
- April 26, 121– March 17, 180

Follow your desire as long as you live and do not perform more than is ordered; do not lessen the time of following desire, for the wasting of time is an abomination to the spirit... When riches are gained, follow desire, for riches will not profit if one is sluggish

- Ptahhotpe
- 2400 BC

Be cheerful while you are alive.

- Ptahhopte
- 2400 BC

Do justice, that you may live long upon earthCalm the weeper, do not oppress the widow, do not oust a man from his father's property, do not degrade magnates from their seats. Beware of punishing wrongfully; do not kill, for it will not profit you.

- Merikare
- 2135 – 2040 BC

Instill the love of you into the world, for a good character is what is remembered.

- Merikare
- 2135 – 2040 BC

The ear of jealousy hear all things

- The Apocrypha (Alexandrine Greek Scripture)

The single best augury is to fight for one's country.

- Homer (the Illiad)
- 700 BC

There is strength in the union even of very sorry men.

- Homer (the Illiad)
- 700 BC

Of men who have a sense of honor, more come through alive than are slain, but from those who flee comes neither glory nor any help.

- Homer (the Illiad)
- 700 BC

You out not to practice childish ways, since you are no longer that age.

- Homer (the Illiad)
- 700 BC

Men flourish for only a moment.

- Homer (the Illiad)
- 700 BC

He who loves the world as his body may be entrusted with the empire.

- Lao tzu
- 604 – 531 BC

He who know others is wise; he who knows himself is enlightened.

- Lao tzu
- 604 – 531 BC

To know that you do not know is the best. To pretend to know when you do not know is a disease.

- Lao tzu
- 604 – 531 BC

Hold faithfulness and sincerity as first principles.

- Confucius
- 551 BC - 479 BC

Have no friends equal to yourself.

- Confucius
- 551 BC - 479 BC

The superior man... does not set his mind either for anything or against anything; what is right he will follow.

- Confucius
- 551 BC - 479 BC

The strong one can escape (?) from anyone's hand.

- Instructions of Shuruppak
- 2600 BC

The man who in the view of gain thinks of righteousness; who in the view of danger is prepared to give up his life; and who does not forget an old agreement, however far back it extends – such a man may be reckoned a complete man.

- Confucius
- 551 BC - 479 BC

He who speaks without modesty will find it difficult to make his words good.

- Confucius
- 551 BC - 479 BC

The superior man is modest in his speech, but exceeds in his actions.

- Confucius
- 551 BC - 479 BC

What the superior mans seeks is in himself. What the mean man seeks is in others.

- Confucius
- 551 BC - 479 BC

What you do not want done to yourself, do not do to others.

- Confucius
- 551 BC - 479 BC

There are three things which the superior man guards against. His youth...lust. When he is strong...quarrelsomeness. When he is old... covetousness.

- Confucius
- 551 BC - 479 BC

Wait for that wisest of all counselors, Time.

- Pericles
- 495-429 BC

There is one thing alone that stands the brunt of life throughout its course: a quiet conscience.

- Euripides
- 485 – 406 BC

In soft regions are born soft men.

- Herodotus
- 485 – 425 BC

There are two sides to every question.

- Protagoras
- 485 – 410 BC

Man is the measure of all things.

- Protagoras
- 485 – 410 BC

Life is short, the art long, opportunity fleeting, experiment treacherous, judgment difficult.

- Hippocrates
- 460 -377 BC

The wise learn many things from their enemies.

- Aristophanes
- 450 – 385 BC

High thoughts must have high language.

- Aristophanes
- 450 – 385 BC

The life which is unexamined is not worth living.

- Plato
- 428 – 348 BC

Nothing is easier than self-deceit. For what each man wishes, that he also believes to be true.

- Demosthenes
- 384 – 322 BC

For all men strive to grasp what they do not know, while none strive to grasp what they already know; and all strive to discredit what they do not excel in, while non strive to discredit what they do excel in. this why there is chaos.

- Chuang-tzu
- 369 – 286 BC

We live, not as we wish to, but as we can.

- Menander
- 342 – 292 BC

Health and intellect are the two blessings of life.

- Menander
- 342 – 292 BC

Conscience is a God to all mortals.

- Menander
- 342 – 292 BC

Practice yourself what you preach.

- Titus Maccius Plautus
- 254 – 184 BC

He is wise who tried everything before arms.

- Terence
- 190 – 159 BC

Happy the man who could search out the causes of things.

- Virgil
- 86 – 34 BC

Force without wisdom falls of its own weight.

- Horace
- 65 – 8 BC

To do two things at once is to do neither.

- Pubilius Syrus
- 1 BC

Never promise more than you can perform.

- Pubilius Syrus
- 1 BC

No man is happy who does not think himself so.

- Pubilius Syrus
- 1 BC

Live among men as if god beheld you; speak to goad as if men were listening.

- Lucius Anneaus Seneca
- 4 BC – 65 AD

You can tell the character of every man when you see how he receives praise.

- Lucius Anneaus Seneca
- 4 BC – 65 AD

A man who is always ready to believe what is told him he will never do well.

- Gaius Petronius
- 66 AD

Sublimity is the echo of a noble mind.

- Longinus
- 1 AD

Tomorrows life is too late. Live today.

- Martial
- 40 -104 AD

Practice yourself, for heaven's sake, in little things; and thence proceed to greater.

- Epictetus
- 55 – 135 AD

First say to yourself what you would be; and then do what you have to do.

- Epictetus
- 55 – 135 AD

Remember you ought to behave in life as you would at a banquet. As something is being passed around it comes to you; stretch out your hand, take a portion of it politely. It passes on; do not detain it. Or it has not come to you yet; do not project your desire to meet it, but wait until it comes in front of you. So act toward children, so toward a wife, so toward office, so toward wealth.

- Epictetus
- 55 – 135 AD

Feelings are great servants but poor masters.

- Doctrine of Ma'at
- 1240 BC

In the morning, when you are sluggish about getting up, let this thought be present: "I am rising to a man's work."

- Marcus Aurelius Antoninus
- 121 – 180 AD

Every day we are changing, every day we are dying, and yet we fancy ourselves eternal.

- Saint Jerome
- 342 – 420 AD

Hear the other side.

- Saint Augustine
- 354 - 430

One must not always think so much about what one should do, but rather what one should be. Our works do not ennoble us; but we must ennoble our works.

- Meister Eckhart
- 1260 – 1327 AD

Whatever advice you give, be brief.

- Horace
- 65 – 8 BC

Mastery of the passions, allows divine thought and action.

- Doctrine of Ma'at
- 1240 BC

First say to yourself what you would be; and then do what you have to do.

- Epictetus
- 100 BC

No one knows what he can do till he tries.

- Publilius Syrus
- 1st century BC

If we let things terrify us, life will not be worth living.

- Seneca
- 54 BC- ca. 39 AD

Only the just man enjoys peace of mind.

- Epicurus
- 300 BC

He who stands on his tiptoes does not stand firm.

- Lao Tzu
- 6th Century BC

The worst of all deceptions is self-deception.

- Plato
- 4th Century BC

The aim of the superior man is truth.

- Confucius
- 551 BC - 479 BC

You should not boast; then your words will be trusted.

- Instructions of Shuruppak
- 2600 BC

Force without wisdom fall of its own weight.

- Horace
- 1st Century BC

Without friends, no one would chose to live, though he had all the Gods.

- Aristotle
- 384 BC – 322 BC

In ancient times, men learned with a view toward their own improvement. Nowadays, men learn with a view towards the approbation of others.

- Confucius
- 551 BC - 479 BC

The sum of things is ever being renewed, and mortals live dependent upon one another. Some nations increase, others diminish and in a short space the generations of living creatures are changed and like runners pass on the torch of life.

- Lucretius
- 99 BC- ca. 55 BC

Great is Truth, and mighty above all things.

- The Apocrypha (Alexandrine Greek Scripture)

A young man is embarrassed to question an older one.

- Homer (the Illiad)
- 850 BC

A journey of a thousand miles must begin with a single step.

- Lao tzu
- 604 – 531 BC

The Gods help them that help themselves.

- Aesop
- 550 BC

War spares not the brave, but the cowardly.

- Anacreon
- 570 - 480 BC

A youth, when at home, should be filial, and abroad, respectful to his elders.

- Confucius
- 551 BC - 479 BC

Man is born for uprightness. If a man lose his uprightness, and yet live, his escape from death is effect of mere good fortune.

- Confucius
- 551 BC - 479 BC

The relation between superiors and inferiors is like that between the wind and the grass. The grass must bend when the wind blows across it.

- Confucius
- 551 BC - 479 BC

The descent to Hades is the same from every place.

- Anaxagoras
- 500 – 428 BC

Time is the most valuable thing a man can spend.

- - Theophrastus
- - 278 BC

I would much rather have men ask why I have no statue, than why I have one.

- - Cato the Elder
- - 234 – 149 BC

You should not pass judgment when you drink beer.

- - Instructions of Shuruppak
- - 2600 BC

Life is one long struggle in the dark.

- - Lucretius
- - 99 – 55 BC

In adversity, remember to keep an open mind.

- - Horace
- - 65 – 8 BC

The secret of happiness is freedom, and the secret of freedom, courage.

- - Thucydides
- - 429 BC

Nobody becomes guilty by fate.

- Seneca
- 54 BC- ca. 39 AD

The nature of men is always the same, it is their habits that separate them.

- Confucius
- 551 BC - 479 BC

What is done well is done quickly enough.

- August Caesar
- 100 AD

Haste in every business brings failures.

- Herodotus
- 5th century BC

More haste, less speed.

- Theognis
- 6th century BC

I detest that man who hides one thing in the depth of his heart and speaks forth another.

- Homer
- 8th century BC

When a judge sits in judgment over a fellow man, he should feel as if a sword is pointed at his own heart.

- Talmud
- 6th Century

Those who God wishes to destroy, he makes mad.

- Euripides
- 400 BC

To fight and conquer in all your battles is not supreme excellence; supreme excellence consists in breaking the enemy's resistance without fighting.

- Sun Tzu
- 4th Century BC

Live life, and not shall you die.

- Doctrine of Ma'at
- 1240 BC

Prayer indeed is good but while calling on the gods, a man should himself lend a hand.

- Hippocrates
- 400 BC

Learn what you are and be such.

- Pindar
- 5th Century

Endure and preserve yourselves for better things.

- Virgil
- 19 BC

Those who go overseas find a change of climate, not a change of soul.

- Horace
- 20 BC

Speak no evil of an absent friend.

- Plautus
- 190 BC

Admonish your friends in private; praise them in pubic.

- Publilus Syrus
- 50 BC

Be master of thy anger.

- Periander of Corinth
- 600 BC

Every man is like the company her keeps.

- Euripides
- 410 BC

The wise man will want to be ever with him who is better than himself.

- Plato
- 360 BC

The body becomes what the foods are, the spirit becomes what the thoughts are.

- - Doctrine of Ma'at
- - 1240 BC

Comparisons are odious.

- - John Fortescue
- - 1462 AD

To know what is right and not to do it is the worst cowardice.

- - Confucius
- - 500 BC

If a son strike his father, his hands shall be hewn off.

- - The Code of Hammurabi
- - 1760 BC

Do not envy the wealth of your neighbor.

- - Homer
- - 800 BC

Noble fathers have noble children.

- - Euripides
- - 425 BC

Fierce eagles do not produce timorous doves.

- Horace
- 13 BC

The intention makes the crime.

- Aristotle
- 322 BC

In honorable dealing we must consider what we intended, not what we said.

- Cicero
- 78 BC

To mean well is nothing without to do well.

- Plautus
- 190 BC

My son, you should not sit alone in a chamber with a married woman.

- Instructions of Shuruppak
- 2600 BC

Labor conquers all things.

- Virgil
- 30 BC

Live with men as if God saw you; converse with God as if men heard you.

- Seneca
- 63 BC

To be a slave to pleasure is the life of a harlot, not of a man.

- Anaxandrides
- 376 BC

In the Book of Poetry there are three hundred poems, but the meaning of all of them may be put in a single sentence: Have no debasing thoughts.

- Confucius
- 500 BC

God lends a helping hand to the man who tries hard.

- Aeschylus
- 490 BC

Shame is the mark of a base man, and belongs to a character capable of shameful acts.

- Aristotle
- 340 BC

Speech is the mirror of the soul; as a man speaks, so he is.

- Publilius Syrus
- 50 BC

The aim of the superior man is truth.

- Confucius
- 500 BC

Let you every act and word and thought be those of a man ready to depart from life this moment.

- Marcus Aurelius
- 100 AD

Golden Rule

Do not to your neighbor what you would take ill from him.

- Pittacus
- 640 BC

Avoid doing what you would blame others for doing.

- Thales
- 624 BC

Do not do to others what would anger you if done to you by others.

- Isocrates
- 436 BC

What thou avoidest suffering thyself seek not to impose on others.

- Epictetus
- 55 AD

It is impossible to live a pleasant life without living wisely and well and justly and it is impossible to live wisely and well and justly without living a pleasant life.

- Epicurus
- 340 BC

One who, while himself seeking happiness, oppresses with violence other beings who also desire happiness, will not attain happiness hereafter.

- Buddhaghosa (attributed)
- 400 AD

Never impose on others what you would not choose for yourself.

- Confucius
- 500 BC

One should never do that to another which one regards as injurious to one's own self.

- Mahabharata
- 800 BC

Hurt no one so that no one may hurt you.

- Muhammad
- 570 AD

In support of this Truth, I ask you a question - "Is sorrow or pain desirable to you ?" If you say "yes it is", it would be a lie. If you say, "No, It is not" you will be expressing the truth. Just as sorrow or pain is not desirable to you, so it is to all which breathe, exist, live or have any essence of life. To you and all, it is undesirable, and painful, and repugnant.

- Acaranga Sutra
- 800 BC (Approximate)

That which is hateful to you, do not do to your fellow. That is the whole Torah; the rest is the explanation; go and learn.

- Hillel the Elder
- 100 BC (approximate)

The sage has no interest of his own, but takes the interests of the people as his own. He is kind to the kind; he is also kind to the unkind: for Virtue is kind. He is faithful to the faithful; he is also faithful to the unfaithful: for Virtue is faithful.

- Tao Te Ching
- 600 BC

An enemy should be hated only so far as one may be hated who may one day be a friend.

- Sophocles
- 450 BC

Treat your friend as if he will one day be your enemy, and your enemy as if he will one day be your friend.

- Laberius
- 45 BC

Good and evil do not befall men without reason. Heaven sends them happiness or misery according to their conduct.

- Confucius
- 500 BC

Tse-kung asked, 'Is there one word that can serve as a principle of conduct for life?' Confucius replied, 'It is the word 'shu' -- reciprocity. Do not impose on others what you yourself do not desire.

- Confucius
- 500 BC

Do for one who may do for you, that you may cause him thus to do.

- The Tale of the Eloquent Peasant
- 1800 BC

None of you [truly] believes until he wishes for his brother what he wishes for himself.

- Al-Nawawi's Forty Hadiths (by Yahya ibn Sharaf al-Nawawi)
- 1200 AD

It is not difficult to govern. All one has to do is not to offend the noble families.

- Mencius
- 372 – 289 BC

Zeus does not bring all men's plans to fulfillment.

- Homer (the Illiad)
- 850 BC

People are difficult to govern because they have too much knowledge.

- Lao tzu
- 604 – 531 BC

The people may be made to follow a path of action, but they may not be made to understand it.

- Confucius
- 551 BC - 479 BC

For deadly blow let him pay with a deadly blow: it is for him who has done a deed to suffer.

- Aeschylus
- 525 – 456 BC

Convention is the ruler of all.

- Pindar
- 518 – 438 BC

Men trust their ears less than their eyes.

- Herodotus
- 485 – 425 BC

The best political community is formed by citizens of the middle class.

- Aristotle
- 984 – 322 BC

The man who runs may fight again.

- Menander
- 342 – 292 BC

You know how to win a victory, Hannibal, but not how to use it.

- Mararbal
- 210 BC

Extreme law is often extreme injustice.

- Terence
- 190 – 159 BC

Each of us bears his own Hell.

- Virgil
- 86 – 34 BC

An old story, but the glory of it is forever.

- Virgil
- 86 – 34 BC

He who has begun has half done. Dare to be wise; begin.

- Horace
- 65 – 8 BC

God changes not what is in a people, until they change what is in themselves.

- The Koran (Qur'an)
- 570 – 632

Give me today, and take tomorrow.

- Saint Chrysostom
- 347 AD

Let justice be done though the heavens may fall.

- Lucius
- 43 BC

The more wise and powerful a master, the more directly is his work created and the simpler it is.

- Meister Eckhart
- 1260 – 1327 AD

The greatest thing in style is to have command of metaphor.

- Aristotle
- 400 BC

Nothing is permanent but change.

- Heraclitus
- 4th century BC

When one prefers ones own children to the children of others, war is near.

- Mahabharata
- 800 BC

Death is nothing to us, since when we are, death has not come, and when death has come, we are not.

- Epicurus
- 3rd century BC

One must learn by doing the thing; through you think you know it, you have no certainty until you try.

- Sophocles
- 5th century BC

We often give our enemies the means of our own destruction.

- Aesop
- 6th century BC

A leader is best, when people hardly know that he exists. Not so good when people obey and acclaim him. Worst when they despise him.

- Lao Tzu
- 6th century BC

Man is a wolf to man.

- Plautus
- 200 BC

Laws are like spiders webs: If some poor weak creature comes up against them, it is caught; but a big one can break through and get away.

- Solon
- 6th Century BC

Beyond his strength no man can fight, though eager.

- Homer
- 8th century BC

The true creator is necessity, which is the mother of our invention.

- Plato
- 4th Century BC

No one loves his country for its size or eminence, but because it is his own.

- Seneca
- 1st century BC

Certain peace is better than anticipated victory.

- Livy
- 14 AD

They make a desert and call it peace.

- Tacitus
- 98 AD

Reason can wrestle and overthrow terror.

- Euripides
- 405 BC

They can do all because they think they can.

- Virgil
- 19 BC

If I am not for myself, who is for me?

- Hillel "the Elder"
- 30 BC – 9 AD

The desire for fame tempts even noble minds.

- St. Augustine
- 415 AD

Amid the suffering of life on earth, suicide is Gods best gift to man.

- Pliny
- 77 AD

Union gives strength.

- Aesop
- 6th Century BC

The loser is always suspicious.

- Publilus Syrus
- 1st Century BC

It is best to win without fighting.

- Sun Tze
- 4th Century BC

Wisdom comes only through suffering.

- Aeschylus
- 5th Century BC

The way of the sage is to act, but not to compete.

- Lao Tzu
- 6th Century BC

What is work? And what is not work? These are questions that perplex the wisest of men.

- Bhagavad Gita
- 250 BC

All composite things decay. Strive diligently.

- Buddha
- 483 BC

They are able, because they think they are able.

- Virgil
- 19 BC

Even the best pilots are willing to take advice from their passengers in bad weather.

- Cicero
- 60 BC

The strength of an army lies in the strict discipline and undeviating obedience to its officers.

- Thucydides
- 410 BC

No one has ever died an atheist.

- Plato
- 360 BC

The man whose authority is recent is always stern.

- Aeschylus
- 490 BC

We believe whatever we want to believe.

- Demosthenes
- 348 BC

The coward calls himself cautious.

- Publilius Syrus
- 50 BC

If conspirators meet in the house of a tavern-keeper, and these conspirators are not captured and delivered to the court, the tavern-keeper shall be put to death.

- The Code of Hammurabi
- 1760 BC

Debt is the slavery of the free.

- Publilus Syrus
- 50 BC

Think long when you may decide only once.

- Publilus Syrus
- 50 BC

The reward of suffering is experience.

- Seschylus
- 490 BC

Fortune can take from us nothing but what she gave us.

- Publilus Syrus
- 50 BC

Adversity reveals the genius of a general; good fortune conceals it.

- Horace
- 25 BC

History repeats itself.

- Thucydides
- 410 BC

Be not long away from home.

- Homer
- 850 BC

A host is like a general: it takes a mishaps to reveal his genius.

- Horace
- 25 BC

I am a man; and nothing human is foreign to me.

- Terence
- 160 BC

A hungry stomach will not allow its owner to forget it, what his cares and sorrows.

- Homer
- 850 BC

Without the hope of immortality no one would ever face death for his country.

- Cicero
- 45 BC

Impulse manages everything badly.

- Statius
- 45 AD

The injury we do and the one we suffer are not weighed in the same scales.

- Aesop
- 600 BC

The pleasantest laughter is at the expense of our enemies.

- Sophocles
- 450 BC

Laws, like cobwebs, entangle the weak, but are broken by the strong.

- Solon
- 575 BC

The purpose of law is to prevent the strong always having their way.

- Dionysius of Halicarnassus
- 20 BC

The lion does not always feast. Strong though he be, he does sometimes fears hunger.

- Theognis
- 550 BC

It is hard to have pity and be wise.

- Agesilaus
- 438 BC

Seek to perform your duties to your highest ability, this way your actions will be blameless.

- Doctrine of Ma'at
- 1240 BC

What is food to one man may be poison to another.

- Lucretius
- 57 BC

Practice is everything.

- Periander of Corinth
- 600 BC

The sweetest of all sounds is praise.

- Zenophon
- 373 BC

Pray, for all men need the aid of the gods.

- Homer
- 500 BC

God does not listen to the prayer of the lazy.

- Pope Xystus
- 150 AD

To lean an untrained people to war is to throw them away.

- Confucius
- 500 BC

Three sparks kindle in all hearts – pride, envy, and avarice.

- Dante
- 1320 AD

All develops upward, anything that opposes the upward movement is destroyed.

- Doctrine of Ma'at
- 1240 BC

The desire to have things done quickly prevents their being done thoroughly.

- Confucius
- 500 BC

No man will be respected by others who is despised by his own relatives.

- Plautus
- 190 BC

Too much liberty leads both men and nations to slavery.

- Cicero
- 50 BC

When soldiers run away in war they never blame themselves: they blame their general of their fellow-soldiers.

- Demosthenes
- 348 BC

The gods always favor the strong.

- Tacitus
- 110 AD

If you are skilled in the art of speech, you will prevail; the tongue is a leaders sword; speaking rightly is more powerful than all fighting. The skillful speech cannot be overcome.

- Doctrine of Ma'at (Stele of Djehuti-Nefer)
- 1240 BC

The sword is the protector of all.

- Seneca
- 50 AD

Second thoughts are the wisest.

- Euripides
- 428 BC

There is nothing doesn't by the hands of man which sometime or other does not destroy.

- Cicero
- 46 BC

Traitors are disliked even by those they favor.

- Tacitus
- 100 AD

Victory often changes her side.

- Homer
- 805 BC

It is no doubt a good thing to conquer on the field of battle, but it needs greater wisdom and greater skill to make use of victory.

- Polybius
- 125 BC

Hannibal knew how to gain a victory, but not how to use it.

- Plutarch
- 100 AD

Men grow tired of sleep, love, singing and dancing sooner than war.

- Homer
- 800 BC

Wine is the first weapon that devils us in attacking the young.

- St Jerome
- 420 AD

The best way to victory is when the opponent surrenders of its own accord before there are any actual hostilities...It is best to win without fighting.

- Sun-tzu
- 722–481 BC

Truth and knowledge produce courage.

- Doctrine of Ma'at
- 1240 BC

Love

When the candles are out, all women are fair.

- Plutarch
- 46 AD - 120 AD

Therefore don't you be gentle to your wife either. Don't tell her everything you know, but tell her one thing and keep another thing hidden.

- Homer (the Illiad)
- 700 BC

There is no more virtue in trusting women.

- Homer (the Illiad)
- 700 BC

The wine urges me on, the bewitching wine, which sets even a wise man to singing and to laughing gently and rouses him up to dance and brings fourth words which were better unspoken.

- Homer (the Illiad)
- 700 BC

Your heart is always harder than stone.

- Homer (the Illiad)
- 700 BC

Use it and you will never wear it out.

- Lao tzu
- 604 – 531 BC

For hatred does not cease by hatred at any time: hatred ceases by love – this is the eternal law.

- The Pali Canon
- 500 – 250 BC

One word, frees us of all weight and pain of life. That word is love.

- Sophocles
- 495 – 406

A woman takes off her claim to respect along with her garments.

- Herodotus
- 485 – 425 BC

There is no animal more invincible than a woman, nor fire either, nor any wildcat so ruthless.

- Aristophanes
- 450 – 385 BC

There's nothing worse in the world than shameless woman – save some other woman.

- Aristophanes
- 450 – 385 BC

No guest is so welcome in a friends house that he will not become a nuisance after three days.

- Titus Maccius Plautus
- 254 – 184 BC

Who sees Me in all, And sees all in me, For him I am not lost and he is not lost for Me.

- Bhagavad Gita
- 250 – BC

Love conquers all things; let us too surrender to love.

- Virgil
- 70 – 19 BC

A woman is always fickle, unstable thing.

- Virgil
- 86 – 34 BC

Every lover is a warrior, and Cupid has his camps.

- Ovid
- 43 – 18 BC

To be loved, be loveable.

- Ovid
- 43 – 18 BC

So long as you are secure you will cont many friends; if your life becomes clouded you will be alone.

- Ovid
- 43 – 18 BC

If what is hateful to you do not do to your neighbor. That is the whole Torah. The rest is commentary.

- Hilel
- 30 BC – 10 AD

How much time he gains who does not look to see what his neighbor say or does or thinks, but only at what he does himself, to make it just and holy.

- Marcus Aurelius Antoninus
- 121 – 180 AD

Love with little trade which you have learned, and be content with it.

- Marcus Aurelius Antoninus
- 121 – 180 AD

It is man's peculiar duty to love even those who wrong him.

- Marcus Aurelius Antoninus
- 121 – 180 AD

It is easier to mend neglect than to quicken love.

- Saint Jerome
- 342 – 420 AD

Love knows nothing of order.

- Saint Jerome
- 342 – 420 AD

I was in love with nothing.

- Saint Augustine
- 354 – 430

Give me chastity and continence, but not just now.

- Saint Augustine
- 354 - 430

Anger is a week; hate is the tree.

- Saint Augustine
- 354 - 430

Thou has endowed man with the wisdom to relieve the suffering of his brother, to recognize his disorder, to extract the healing substance, to discover their powers and to apply them to suit every ill.

- Maimonides
- 1135 – 1204 AD

Be not angry that you cannot make others as you wish them to be, since you cannot make yourself as you wish to be.

- Thomas a Kempis
- 1380 – 1471 AD

And when he is out of sight, quickly also is he out of mind.

- Thomas a Kempis
- 1380 – 1471 AD

Love blinds all men alike, both the reasonable and the foolish.

- Menander
- 4th BC

Love is a kind of warefare.

- Ovid
- 2 BC

One word frees us of all the weight and pain of life: That word is love.

- Sophocles
- 5th Century BC

Love conquers all: and let us too surrender to love.

- Virgil
- 37 BC

Whether a pretty woman grants or withholds her favors, she always likes to be asked for them.

- Ovid
- 43 BC – 17 AD

No pleasure lasts long unless there is variety in it.

- Publilus Syrus
- 1st Century BC

Wherever women are honored, there the Gods are pleased.

- Code of Manu
- 100 BC

By now, you will have discovered that women too, can be militant.

- Sophocles
- 5th Century BC

I can't live either with you or without you.

- Ovid
- 20 BC

He who has a thousand friends has not a friend to spare, and he who has one enemy will meet him everywhere.

- Ali Ibn-Abi-Talib
- 7th century BC

Pay attention to your foes, for they are the first to discover your mistakes.

- Antisthenes
- 3rd century BC

Where there's life, there's hope.

- Terence
- 163 BC

Nature is not human-hearted.

- Lao Tzu
- 6th Century BC

Happy that man whose children make his happiness in life and not his grief.

- Euripides
- 408 BC

Happy is he who learns the causes of things.

- Virgil
- 70 – 19 BC

No act of kindness, no matter how small, is ever wasted.

- Aesop
- 6th Century BC

Pay attention to the young, and make them just as good as possible.

- Socrates
- 5th Century BC

A youth is to be regarded with respect. How do you know is future will not be equal to your present.

- Confucius
- 6th Century BC

Such is the way of the adulterous woman; she eateth, and wipeth her mouth, and saith, I have done no wickedness.

- Proverbs 350 BC
- 350 BC

The best cure for anger is delay.

- Seneca
- 43 AD

What is beautiful is good, and who is good will soon be beautiful.

- Sappho
- 610 BC

Beauty is a frail good.

- Ovid
- 2 BC

If the wife hath beauty, the whole house is bright, but if she lack it all will appear dismal.

- The Code of Manu
- 100 AD

The five blessings are long life, riches, serenity, the love of virtue, and the attainment of ambition.

- The Hung-Fan
- 1100 BC

When conscience discovers nothing wrong, what is there to be uneasy about, what is there to fear?

- Confucius
- 500 BC

The covetous man is full of fear; and he who lives in fear will ever be a bondman.

- Horace
- 20 BC

To confess a fault freely is the next thing to being innocent of it.

- Publilus Syrus
- 50 BC

Comparisons turn friends into enemies.

- Philemon
- 310 BC

If a man take a woman to wife, but have no intercourse with her, this woman is no wife to him.

- The Code of Hammurabi
- 1760 BC

If a woman quarrel with her husband, and say: "You are not congenial to me," the reasons for her prejudice must be presented. If she is guiltless, and there is no fault on her part, but he leaves and neglects her, then no guilt attaches to this woman, she shall take her dowry and go back to her father's house.

- The Code of Hammurabi
- 1760BC

A wife must worship her husband as if he were a god, though he may be without virtue or other good qualities, and seek pleasure with other women.

- The Code of Manu
- 100 AD

Journeys end in lovers meeting.

- Shakespeare
- 1500

Wherever there is a human being there is a chance for kindness.

- Seneca
- 60 AD

Better is a dinner of herbs where love is, than a stalled ox and hatred therewith.

- Proverbs
- 350 BC

Can there be a love which does not make demands on its object?

- Confucius
- 500 BC

At the touch of love every one becomes a poet.

- Plato
- 360 BC

Even a god, falling in love, could not be wise.

- Publilius Syrus
- 50 BC

Let the man who does not wish to be idle fall in love.

- Publilius Syrus
- 50 BC

In love, pain and pleasure are always at war.

- Publilius Syrus
- 50 BC

He is not a lover who does not love forever.

- Euripides
- 415 BC

The quarrels of lovers are the renewal of love.

- Terence
- 160 BC

Jupiter laughs at the perjuries of lovers.

- Ovid
- 2BC

Lovers remember everything.

- Ovid
- 2 BC

The less my hope the warmer my love.

- Terence
- 160 BC

So long as a man desires women his mind is in bondage, as if a calf is in bondage to its mother.

- The Dhammapada
- 100 AD

Marriage lies at the bottom of all government.

- Confucius
- 500 BC

There is no such thing as pure pleasure; some anxiety always goes with it.

- Ovid
- 5 AD

A prostitute is a furnace of love, burning youth and money.

- Bhartrihari
- 625 AD

Women have learned to shed tears in order that they may lie the better.

- Publilius Syrus
- 50 BC

No pleasure lasts long unless there is variety in it.

- Publilius Syrus
- 50 BC

No trust is to be placed in women.

- Homer
- 800 BC

There is no fouler fiend than a woman when her mind is bent to evil.

- Homer
- 800 BC

Nature has given horns to bulls, hoofs to horses, swiftness to hared, the power of swimming to fishes, of flying to birds, understanding to men. She had nothing more for women.

- Anacreon
- 500 BC

Silence gives the proper grace to women.

- Sophocles
- 450 BC

The best ornaments of a woman are silence and modesty.

- Euripides
- 420 BC

A woman finds it much easier to do ill than well.

- Plautus
- 190 BC

I know the ways of women: they won't when though wilt, and when though won't they are passionately fond.

- Terence
- 160 BC

The vows that woman makes to her lover are only fit to be written on air.

- Catullius
- 60 BC

A woman either loves or hates; she knows no medium.

- Publilius Syrus
- 50 BC

In evil counsel women always beat men.

- Publilius Syrus
- 50 BC

You should make a woman angry if you wish her to love.

- Publilius Syrus
- 50 BC

A woman is always buying something.

- Ovid
- 2 BC

Wherever women are honored, there the gods are pleased.

- The Code of Manu
- 100 AD

Woman is the chain by which man is attached to the chariot of folly.

- Bharatrihari
- 625 AD

Nothing enchants the soul so much as young women. They alone are the cause of evil, and there is no other.

- Bhartrihari
- 625 AD

Remember you aret man's reasonable companion, not the slave of his passion; the end of they being is not merely to gratify his loose desire, but to assist him in the toils of life, to soothe him with they tenderness, and recompense his care and like treatment with soft endearments.

- Doctrine of Ma'at
- 1240 BC

Money

Money alone sets all the world in motion.

- Publlius

We all line in a state of ambitious poverty.

- Juvenal

We are just statistics, born to consume resources.

- Horace
- 65 BC - 8 BC

Even though work stops, expenses run on.

- Cato the Elder
- 264 BC

The stink of profit is sweet, whatever its source.

- Juvenal
- 1 AD

He has not acquired a fortune, the fortune has acquired him.

- Bion
- 325-c. 250 BC

We must have richness of the soul.

- Antiphanes
- 408 to 334 BC

To want nothing is Godlike, and the less we want, the nearer we approach the divine.

- Xenophon
- 431 – 355 BC

The shifts of fortune tests the reliability of friends.

- Cicero
- 106 BC – 43 BC

Better is bread with a happy heart; than wealth with vexation.

- Amenemope
- 1100 BC

To have plenty is to be perplexed.

- Lao tzu
- 604 – 531 BC

When opulence and extravagance are a necessity instead of righteousness and truth, society will be governed by greed and injustice.

- Doctrine of Ma'at
- 1240 BC

There is no greater guild that discontentment. And there is no greater disaster than greed.

- Lao tzu
- 604 – 531 BC

One finds many companions for food and drink, but in a serious business a man's companions are very few.

- Theognis
- 545 BC

No man takes with him to Hades all his exceeding wealth.

- Theognis
- 545 BC

Of all human ills, greatest is fortunes wayward tyranny.

- Sophocles
- 495 – 406

Money: There's nothing in the world so demoralizing as money.

- Sophocles
- 495 – 406

A mans homeland is wherever he prospers.

- Aristophanes
- 450 – 385 BC

The good have no need of an advocate.

- Phocion
- 402 – 317

Wealth is the sinews of affairs.

- Bion
- 325 – 255 BC

He has not acquired a fortune; the fortune has acquired him.

- Bion
- 325 – 255 BC

Patience is the best remedy for every trouble.

- Titus Maccius Plautus
- 254 – 184 BC

One is never so happy as when giving happiness unto others.

- Doctrine of Ma'at
- 1240 BC

Consider the little mouse, how sagacious an animal it is which never entrusts its life to one hold only.

- Titus Maccius Plautus
- 254 – 184 BC

Even though work stops, expenses run on.

- Cato the Elder
- 234 – 149 BC

Those who know how to win are much more numerous than those who know how to make proper use of their victories.

- Polybius
- 200 – 118 BC

But if one should guide his life by true principles, man's greatest riches is to live on a little with contented mind; for a little is never lacking.

- Lucretius
- 99 – 55 BC

Ambition drove many men to become false; to have one though locked in the breast, another ready on the tongue.

- Sallust
- 86 – 34 BC

In truth, prosperity tries the souls even of the wise.

- Sallust
- 86 – 34 BC

We rarely find anyone who can say he has lived a happy life, and who, content with his life, can retire from the world like a satisfied guest.

- Horace
- 65 – 8 BC

Be industrious, let thin eyes be open, lest you become a beggar, for the man that is idle cometh not to honor.

- Doctrine of Ma'at
- 1240 BC

It is not the rich man you should properly call happy, but him who knows how to use with wisdom the blessings of the gods, to endure hard poverty, and who fears dishonor worse than death, and it not afraid to die for cherished friends or fatherland.

- Horace
- 65 – 8 BC

Make money, money by fair means if you can, if not, by any means money.

- Horace
- 65 – 8 BC

The covetous man is ever in want.

- Horace
- 65 – 8 BC

Money alone sets all the world in motion.

- Pubilius Syrus
- 1 BC

The more flesh, the more worms. The more possessions, the more worry.

- Hilel
- 30 BC – 10 AD

The best ideas are common property.

- Lucius Anneaus Seneca
- 4 BC – 65 AD

No one becomes depraved in a moment.

- Juvenal
- 55 – 130 AD

Bitter poverty has no harder and than that is makes men ridiculous.

- Juvenal
- 55 – 130 AD

The desire for glory clings even to the best men longer than any other passion.

- Cornelius Tacitus
- 56 – 120 AD

The gods are on the side of the stronger.

- Cornelius Tacitus
- 56 – 120 AD

Think of your forefathers and posterity.

- Cornelius Tacitus
- 56 – 120 AD

Everything that is hard to attain is easily assailed by the generality of men.

- Ptolemy (Claudius Ptolemaeus)
- 100 – 178

Avoid, as you would the plague, a clergyman who is also a man of business.

- Saint Jerome
- 342 – 420 AD

One would grow poor staying in one place always.

- Poem of Cid
- 1200 AD

Many receive advice, few profit by it.

- Publilius Syrus
- 1st century BC

Fortune sides with him who dares.

- Virgil
- 19 BC

Much effort, much prosperity.

- Euripides
- 4th century BC

Nothing to excess.

- Solon
- 6th century BC

Wise men profit more by fools, than fools by wise men; fo wise men avoid the mistakes of fools, but fools do not imitate the good examples of wise men.

- Cato the Elder
- 234 – 149 BC

God looks at the clean hands, not the full ones.

- Publilius Syrus
- 1st century BC

The lucky person passes for a genius.

- Euripides
- 428 BC

If you want to have perfect conduct, to be free from evil, then above all guard against the vice of greed. Greed is a grievous sickness that has no cure....It parts the wife from the husband. Greed is a compound of all the evils.

- Doctrine of Ma'at
- 1240 BC

A lucky man is rarer than a white cow.

- Juvenal
- 100 AD

Lucky never made a man wise.

- Seneca
- 1st Century AD

Fortune favors the brave.

- Terence
- 161 BC

Money is far more persuasive than logical arguments.

- Euripides
- 431 BC

Money is life to us wretched mortals.

- Hesiod
- 700 BC

He is almost always a slave who cannot live on little.

- Horace
- 35-30 BC

Nothing hurts worse than the loss of money.

- Livy
- 14 AD

Seize the day and put the least possible trust in tomorrow.

- Horace
- 33- 15 BC

The cautious seldom err.

- Confucius
- 551 BC - 479 BC

Every man is the architect of his own fortune.

- Appius Claudisu Caecus
- 300 BC

The wealth of the soul is the only true wealth.

- Lucian
- 2nd Century AD

When men succeed, even their neighbors think them wise.

- Pindar
- 5th Century BC

As a rule, provincial governors seem to think that there are no reputable families in the land except those of other provincial governors.

- Murasaki Shikibu

Envy crawls before the rich.

- Sophocles
- 450 BC

How sweet it is to have people point and say, "There it is."

- Persius
- 60 AD

If fame is to come only after death, I am in no hurry for it.

- Martial

He who is feared by many must fear many.

- Publilus Syrus
- 50 BC

Man's life is ruled by fortune, not by wisdom.

- Cicero
- 45 BC

Every man is the architect of his own fortune.

- Sallust
- 40 BC

He is always a slave who cannot live on little.

- Horace
- 25 BC

It matters not how long you live, but how well.

- Publilius Syrus
- 50 BC

Opportunity has power of all things.

- Sophocles
- 408 BC

It is hard to find the relatives of a poor man.

- Menander
- 300 BC

The rich have a cloak for their ills, but poverty is a transparent and abject.

- Antiphanes
- 350 BC

It is the nature of the poor to hate and envy men of property.

- Plautus
- 200 BC

The advantage of riches is that they enable a man to indulge his passions, and help him to bear up against whatever harm befalls him.

- Herodotus
- 430 BC

If thou art sluggish on arising, let this through occur: I am rising to a mans work.

- Marcus Aurelius
- 170 AD

To carry on war three things are necessary: money, money and yet more money.

- Gian Jacopo Trivulzio
- 60 BC

Wealth is the thing most honored among men, and the source of the greatest power.

- Euripides
- 410 BC

Nothing is more fallacious than wealth. Today it is for thee, tomorrow it is against thee. It arms the eyes of the envious everywhere. It is hostile comrade, a domestic enemy.

- St John Chrysostom
- 388 AD

Where our work is, there let our joy be.

- Tertullian
- 220 AD

You love honor and victory more than money. It really cares next to nothing about money, for it has not yet learned what the lack of it means.

- Aristotle
- 322 BC

Reason is immortal, all else mortal.

- Pythagoras
- 572 BC- 590 BC

Whatever is well said by another, is mine.

- Seneca
- 54 BC- ca. 39 AD

When a building is all about to fall down, all the mice desert it.

- Pliny the Elder
- 23 – August 25, AD 79

In sorrow, thou shalt bring forth Children.

- The Bible
- Exodus

How forcible are the right words.

- The Bible
- Job

There she met sleep, the brother of death.

- Homer (the Illiad)
- 850 BC

Ocean, who is the source of all.

- Homer (the Illiad)
- 850 BC

The fates have given mankind a patient soul.

- Homer (the Illiad)
- 850 BC

Wine, dear boy, and truth... Wine is a peep-hole on a man.

- Alcaeus
- 625- 575 BC

Heaven and Earth are not humane. They regard all things as straw dogs

- Lao tzu
- 604 – 531 BC

Appearances often are deceiving.

- Aesop
- 550 BC

Do not count your chickens before they are hatched.

- Aesop
- 550 BC

Familiarity breeds contempt.

- Aesop
- 550 BC

Bright youth passes swiftly.

- Theognis
- 545 BC

All is in flux, nothings stays still.

- Heraclitus
- 540 – 480 BC

The greatest grief's are those we cause ourselves.

- Sophocles
- 495 – 406

Time eases all things.

- Sophocles
- 495 – 406

When asked late in life why he was studying geometry: If I should not be learning now, when should I be?

- Lacydes
- 241 BC

In fact, nothing is said that has not been said before.

- Terence
- 190 – 159 BC

History is the witness that testifies to the passing of time; it illuminates reality, vitalizes memory, provides guidance in daily life, and brings us tidings of antiquity.

- Marcus Tullius Cicero
- 106 – 43 BC

The first law for the historian is that he shall never dare utter an untruth. The second is that he shall suppress nothing that is true. Moreover, there shall be no suspicion of partiality in his writing, or of malice.

- Marcus Tullius Cicero
- 106 – 43 BC

There were poets before Homer.

- Marcus Tullius Cicero
- 106 – 43 BC

Anger is a short madness.

- Horace
- 65 – 8 BC

You may drive out Nature with a pitchfork, yet she still will hurry back.

- Horace
- 65 – 8 BC

It is when I struggle to be brief that I become obscure.

- Horace
- 65 – 8 BC

If I am not for myself, who is for me? And when I am for myself, what am I? And if not now, when?

- Hilel
- 30 BC – 10 AD

Man is the only one that knows nothing, that can learn nothing without being taught. He can neither speak nor walk nor eat, and in short he can do nothing at the prompting of nature only, but weep.

- Pliny the Elder
- 23 – 29 AD

Appearances to the mind are of four kinds. Things either are what they appear to be; or they neither are, nor appear to be; or they are, and do not appear to be; or they are not, and yet appear to be. Rightly to aim in all these cases is the wise man's tasks.

- Epictetus
- 55 – 135 AD

Each year new consuls and proconsuls are mad; but not every year is a king or a poet born.

- Lucius Annaeus Florus
- 125 AD

Remember that no man loses other life that that which he lives, nor lives other than that which he loses.

-     Marcus Aurelius Antoninus
-     121 – 180 AD

By a tranquil mind I mean nothing else than a mind well ordered.

-     Marcus Aurelius Antoninus
-     121 – 180 AD

The universe is change; our life is what our thoughts make it.

-     Marcus Aurelius Antoninus
-     121 – 180 AD

"let your occupations be few," says the sage, "if you would lead a tranquil life."

-     Marcus Aurelius Antoninus
-     121 – 180 AD

All is ephemeral – fame and the famous as well.

-     Marcus Aurelius Antoninus
-     121 – 180 AD

Nothing happens to anybody which he is not fitted by nature to bear.

-     Marcus Aurelius Antoninus
-     121 – 180 AD

Very little is needed to make a happy life.

- Marcus Aurelius Antoninus
- 121 – 180 AD

Truth persuades by teaching, but does not teach by persuading.

- Tertullian
- 160 – 240 AD

Out of the frying pan into the fire.

- Tertullian
- 160 – 240 AD

One man's religion neither harms nor helps another man.

- Tertullian
- 160 – 240 AD

It is worse still to be ignorant of your ignorance.

- Saint Jerome
- 342 – 420 AD

The scars of other should teach us caution.

- Saint Jerome
- 342 – 420 AD

When the stomach is full, it is easy to talk of fasting.

- Saint Jerome
- 342 – 420 AD

The tired ox treads with a firmer step.

- - Saint Jerome
- - 342 – 420 AD

Never look a gift horse in the mouth

- - Saint Jerome
- - 342 – 420 AD

They will question thee concerning the soul. Say: "The soul is the concern of my Lord, and you have been given of knowledge but a little."

- - The Koran (Qur'an)
- - 570 – 632

I intend to die in a tavern; let the wine be place near my dying mouth, so tht when the choirs of angels come, they may say, "god be merciful to this drinker."

- - Walter Map
- - 1140 – 1210 AD

The flow of the river is ceaseless and its water I never the same. The bubbles that float in the pools, now vanishing, now forming, are not of long duration: so in the world are man and his dwellings... People die in the morning, they' re born in the evening, like foam on the water.

- - Kamo no Chomei
- - 1153 - 1216

An example from the monkey: The higher it climbs, the more you see of its behind.

- Saint Bonaventure
- 1217 – 1274

Had I been present at the creation, I would have given some useful hints for the better ordering of the universe.

- Alfonso X
- 1221 – 1284 AD

In silence man can most readily preserve his integrity.

- Meister Eckhart
- 1260 – 1327 AD

A great flame follows a little spark.

- Dante Alighieri
- 1265 – 1321 AD

O holy simplicity.

- John Huss
- 1372 – 1415 AD

Old age has a great sense of calm and freedom. When the passions have relaxed their hold, you have escaped not from one master but from many.

- Plato
- 428 BC

Nobody loves life like him who is growing old.

- Sophocles
- 496 BC

Of all the animals, the boy is the most unmanageable.

- Plato
- 428 BC

That which is the common to the greatest number has the least care bestowed upon it.

- Aristotle
- 384 BC

In few people is discretion stronger than the desire to tell a good story.

- Murasaki Shikibu
- 1001 – 1015

Custom is king all over.

- Pindar
- 522 BC

Whom the Gods love dies young.

- Menander
- 342 BC

Death is an evil; the gods have so judged; had it been good, they would die.

- Sahhho
- 700 BC

The life so short, the craft so long to learn.

- Hippocrates
- 460 BC

Education is the best provision for old age.

- Aristotle
- 384 BC

The foundation of every stats is the education of its youth.

- Diogenes
- 460 BC

Nothing at all is to be valued, but life should be sweet. You should not serve things; things should serve you. My son, ...

- Instructions of Shuruppak
- 2600 BC

Only the educated are free.

- Epictetus
- 55 BC

Custom adapts itself to expediency.

- Tacitus
- 100 AD

It is certain because it is impossible. (Credo quia impossibile)

- Tertullian
- 200 AD

Man is the only animal that knows nothing, and can learn nothing without being taught.

- Pliny
- 77 AD

Man is the measure of all things, of things that are, that they are, of things that are not, that they are not.

- Protagoras
- 490 BC

When all the desires that enter one's heart are abandoned, then does the mortal become immortal.

- Brihadaranyaka Upanishad
- 800 – 50 0BC

Familiarity breeds contempt.

- Aesop
- 6th Century BC

Too much rest itself becomes a pain.

- Homer
- 8th century BC

All creatures live bewildered.

- Bhagavad gita
- 250 BC

If a person saves one life it is as if he saved the whole world.

- Talmud
- 6th Century AD

There is no great genius without some touch of madness.

- Seneca
- 4 BC

Memory is the treasury and guardian of all things.

- Cicero
- 55 BC

There is always something new out of Africa.

- Pliny the Elder
- 23 – August 25, AD 79

Obedience is the mother of success and the wife of security.

- Aeschylus
- 525 BC

The unexamined life is not worth living.

- Socrates
- 469 BC

A thief is a lion, but after he has been caught, he will be a slave.

- Instructions of Shuruppak
- 2600 BC

A foreigner scarcely counts as a human being for someone of another race.

- Pliny
- 77 AD

Reason is God's crowning gift to man.

- Sophocles
- 469 BC

Rumor is not always wrong.

- Tacitus
- 98 AD

Nothing exists except atoms and empty space; everything else is opinion.

- Democritus
- 460 BC

Everything existing in the universe is the fruit of chance and necessity.

- Democritus
- 460 BC

To free the spirit, control the senses, the reward will be a clear insight.

- Doctrine of Ma'at
- 1240 BC

Manifest plainness; embrace simplicity; reduce selfishness; have a few desires.

- Lao Tzu
- 6th Century BC

Simplicity, most rare in our age.

- Ovid
- 43 BC – 17 AD

Every vice has its excuse ready.

- Publilius Syrus
- 50 BC

Vices can be learnt even without a teacher.

- Seneca
- 50 BC

In solitude, pride quickly creeps in.

- St Jerome
- 400 AD

Time brings all things to pass.

- Aeschylus
- 5th Century BC

Time is the best medicine.

- Ovid
- 1st Century BC

Time bears away all things, even the mind.

- Virgil
- 70 – 19 BC

There is nothing worse for mortals than a wandering life.

- Homer
- 850 BC

Three things are weakening; fear, sin and travel.

- Talmud
- 6th Century BC

If there we no tribulation, there would be no rest; if there were no winder, there would be no summer.

- St John Chrysostom
- 386 AD

Grief teaches the steadiest minds to waver.

- Sophocles
- 469 BC

The greatest grief's are those we cause ourselves.

- Sophocles
- 469 BC

Trust, like the soul, never returns once it is gone.

- Publilius Syrus
- 50 BC

Nature has buried truth at the bottom of the sea.

- Democritus
- 460 BC

Where wisdom is called for, force is of little use.

- Herodotus
- 450 BC

Youth is quick in feeling but weak in judgment.

- Homer
- 850 BC

Bright youth passes swiftly as a thought.

- Theognis
- 6th Century BC

Old people have fewer diseases than the young, but their diseases never leave them.

- Hippocrates
- 400 BC

Let other praise ancient times; I am glad that I was born in these.

- Ovid
- 2 BC

Let appetite obey reason.

- Cicero
- 78 BC

Once a woman has lost her chastity, she will shrink from nothing.

- Tacitus
- 100 AD

It is men who make a city, not walls or ships.

- Thucydides
- 410 BC

Cleverness is not wisdom.

- Euripides
- 410 BC

If any one take over a waste-lying field to make it arable, but is lazy, and does not make it arable, he shall plow the fallow field in the fourth year, harrow it and till it, and give it back to its owner, and for each ten gan (a measure of area) ten gur of grain shall be paid.

- The Code of Hammurabi
- 1760 BC

If any one be too lazy to keep his dam in proper condition, and does not so keep it; if then the dam break and all the fields be flooded, then shall he in whose dam the break occurred be sold for money, and the money shall replace the corn which he has caused to be ruined.

- The Code of Hammurabi
- 1760 BC

Nothing troubles you which you do not desire.

- Publilus Syrus
- 50 BC

We desire most what we ought not to have.

- Publilus Syrus
- 50 BC

No one desires what is not known.

- Publilus Syrus
- 50 BC

There is death in the pot.

- Kings IV
- 500 BC

Drunkenness is simply a voluntary insanity.

- Seneca
- 63 AD

Drunkenness is the ruin of reason. It is premature old age. It is temporary death.

- St Basil
- 375 AD

The potter envies the potter, the carpenter, the carpenter, the poor is jealous of the poor man, the bard of the bard.

- Hesiod
- 700 BC

Those who are envied are never wholly happy.

- Aeschylus
- 490 BC

It is much better to be envied than pitied.

- Herodotus
- 430 BC

Envy is to be overcome by death.

- Horace
- 5 BC

One evil flows from another.

- Terence
- 160 BC

Let exercise come before meals, not after.

- Hippocrates
- 400 BC

For one that dies of natural causes ninety-nine die of the evil eye.

- The Talmud
- 200 AD

Fat men are more likely to die suddenly than the slender.

- Hippocrates
- 400 BC

Let flattery, the handmaid of vice, be kept out of friendship.

- Cicero
- 50 BC

Forbidden things have a secret charm.

- Tacitus
- 100 AD

There is nothing so advantageous to a man as a forgiving disposition.

- Terence
- 160 BC

Frugality is misery in disguise.

- Publilus Syrus
- 50 BC

No one can be so welcome a guest a that he will not annoy his host after three days.

- Plautus
- 205 BC

Habit is overcome by habit.

- Thomas A Kempis
- 1420 AD

No one is happy all his life long.

- Euripides
- 421 BC

We have two ears and only one tongue in order that we may hear more and speak less.

- Diogenes Laertius
- 150 BC

As there are misanthropes or haters of men, so also are there misologistis, or haters of ideas.

- Plato
- 360 BC

To be ignorant even the words of the wise seem foolish.

- Euripides
- 410 BC

A great part of art consists in imitation. For the whole conduct of life is based on this: that we admire in others we want to do ourselves.

- Quintilian
- 90 AD

A cock has great influence on his own dunghill.

- Publilus Syrus
- 50 BC

The best remedy for an injury is to forget it.

- Publilus Syrus
- 50 BC

An inquisitive person is always ill-natured.

- Plautus
- 200 BC

When you go to an inn, let it not be with the feeling that you must have whatever you ask for.

- Confucius
- 500 BC

We should be gentle with those who err, not in will, but in judgment.

- Sophocles
- 450 BC

Men judge the affairs of the other men better than their own.

- Terence
- 160 BC

When my knowledge was small I swelled with pride like an elephant blinded by passion, and it seemed to me that there was nothing I did not know. But when I learned more I became aware of my foolishness, and my excitement subsided.

- Bharthihari
- 625 BC

Life is nothing but a journey to death.

- Seneca
- 44 AD

Memory is the mother of all wisdom.

- Aeschylus
- 490 BC

Memory is the treasury and guardian of all things.

- Cicero
- 80 BC

The merciful man doeth good to is own.

- Proverbs
- 350 BC

Man is by nature fond of novelty.

- Pliny the Elder.
- 79 AD

Be patient, my soul: thou hath suffered worse than this.

- Homer
- 800 BC

Peace is a nursing-mother to the land.

- Hesiod
- 700 BC

Peace becomes mankind, fury is for beasts.

- Ovid
- 2 BC

They shall beat their swords into ploughshares, and their spears into pruning hooks; nation shall not lift up a sword against nation, neither shall they learn war any more.

- Micah
- 700 BC

That sick man does badly who makes his physician his heir.

- Pubilius Syrus
- 50 BC

The most noble and excellent gift of Heaven to man is reason; and of all the enemies that reason has to engage with pleasure is the chief.

- Cicero
- 78 BC

Democritus maintains that there can be no great poet without a spice of madness.

- Cicero
- 78 BC

The man is either crazy, or he is a poet.

- Horace
- 25 BC

Physicians practice only what belongs to their art; mechanics work only at their trade; but learned and unlearned, we all write verse.

- Horace
- 5 BC

Learning to the inexperienced is a poison; eating upon a full stomach is a poison, the society of the vulgar is a poison, a young wife to an old man is a poison.

- The Hitopadesa
- 500 AD

Nothing is more foreign to us Christians than politics.

- Tertullian
- 215 AD

The poor man's wisdom is despised, and his words are not heard.

- Ecclesiastes
- 200 BC

In the eyes of a wise judge, proofs by reasoning are more value than witnesses.

- Cicero
- 50 BC

The property of the lazy and shiftless belongs to those who are willing to face labor and danger.

- Demosthenes
- 351 BC

If a man destroy the eye of another man, they shall destroy his eye.

- The code of Hammurabi
- 2250 BC

The good and the wise leave quiet lives.

- Euripides
- 420 BC

The very same acts, according as they proceed from a person of a high or low rank, are either much extolled or left unnoticed.

- Pliny the Younger
- 110 AD

Reason is the mistress and queen of all things.

- Cicero
- 45 BC

Dreadful indeed are the feuds of relatives, and difficult the reconciliation.

- Euripides
- 410 BC

Nothing is ever said that has not been said before.

- Terence
- 160 BC

The desire for safety stands against every great and noble enterprise.

- Tacitus
- 110 AD

If you would wish another to keep your secret, first keep it to yourself.

- Seneca
- 60 AD

The more we deny to ourselves, the more gods supply our wants.

- Horace
- 20 BC

I regret that I have spoken; never that I have been silent.

- Publilius Syrus
- 50 BC

God has given to a man cloak whereby he can conceal his ignorance, and in this cloak he can enwrap himself at any moment, for it always lies near his hand. This cloak is silence.

- Bhartrihari
- 625 AD

There is no greater delight than to be conscious of sincerity.

- Mencius
- 300 BC

When a wise man chooses a fit subject he always speaks well.

- Euripides
- 410 BC

Temperance is the moderating of one's desires in obedience to reason.

- Cicero
- 50 BC

No duty is more urgent than that of returning thanks.

- St Ambrose
- 380 BC

Spending time is the theatres produces fornication, intemperance, and every kind of impurity.

- St John Chrysostom
- 388 AD

It is a miserable job to dig a well while you are thirsty.

- Plautus
- 200 BC

Time will reveal everything. It is a babbler, and speaks even when not asked.

- Euripides
- 425 BC

Time will bring to light whatever is hidden, and it will conceal and cover up what is now shining with the greatest splendor.

- Horace
- 5 BC

Time heals what reason cannot.

- Seneca
- 60 AD

Trust to time: it is the wisest of all counselors.

- Plutarch
- 100 AD

The happier the time, the faster it goes.

- Pliny the Younger
- 100 AD

Time and tide wait for no man.

- Chaucer (Attributed)
- 1386 AD

Today is the pupil of yesterday.

- Publilius Syrus
- 50 BC

Tomorrow will give us something to think about.

- Cicero
- 50 BC

A pleasant companion reduces the length of the journey.

- Publilius Syrus
- 50 BC

Travel only with they equals or thy betters; if there are none, travel alone.

- The Dhammapana
- 200 AD

Three things are weakening: fear, sin, and travel.

- The Talmud
- 200 AD

If there were no tribulation, there would be no rest; if there were no Winter, there would be no summer.

- St. John Chrysostom
- 388 AD

The way of truth is like a great highway. It is not hard to find.

- Mencisu
- 300 BC

What hinder one from smiling when speaking the truth?

- Horace
- 25 BC

A thing is worth whatever the buyer will pay for it.

- Publilius Syrus
- 50 BC

The superior man thinks always of virtue; the common man thinks of comfort.

- Confucius
- 500 BC

Five things constitute perfect virtue: gravity, magnanimity, earnestness, sincerity, kindness.

- Confucius
- 500 BC

The human voice is nothing but flogged air.

- Seneca
- 63 AD

Better is it that though shouldest not vow, than that though shouldest vow and not pay.

- Ecclesiastes
- 200 BC

No one is wicked that he wants to seem wicked.

- Quintilian
- 90 AD

Wine gives strength to weary men.

- Homer
- 800 BC

Boys should abstain from all use of wine until their eighteenth year, for it is wrong to add fire to fire.

- Plato
- 360 BC

Those who jest with good taste are called witty.

- Aristotle
- 340 BC

Youth is quick in temper but weak in judgment.

- Homer
- 500 BC

Not have I diminished from the weight of the balance.

- Doctrine of Ma'at
- 1240 BC

Not have I spoken lies. Not have I set my mouth in motion [against any man].

- Doctrine of Ma'at
- 1240 BC

I have not oppressed the members of my family.

- Doctrine of Ma'at
- 1240 BC

I have not wrought evil in the place of right and truth.

- Doctrine of Ma'at
- 1240 BC

I have not done that which is an abomination unto the gods.

- Doctrine of Ma'at
- 1240 BC

Self knowledge is the basis of true knowledge.

- Doctrine of Ma'at
- 1240 BC

The purpose of human life is to achieve a state of consciousness apart form bodily concerns.

- Doctrine of Ma'at
- 1240 BC

Men and women are to become God-like through a life of virtue and the cultivation of the spirit through scientific knowledge, practice and bodily discipline.

- Doctrine of Ma'at
- 1240 BC

The closer you get to truth, the simpler it is.

- Doctrine of Ma'at
- 1240 BC

When the heavenly gods created human beings, they kept everlasting life for themselves and gave us death. So, Gilgamesh, accept your fate. Each day, wash your head, bathe your body, and wear clothes that are sparkling fresh. Fill your stomach with tasty food. Play, sing, dance, and be happy both day and night. Delight in the pleasures that your wife brings you, and cherish the little child who holds your hand. Make every day of your life a feast of rejoicing! This is the task that the gods have set before all human beings. This is the life you should seek, for this is the best life a mortal can hope to achieve.

- Epic of Gilgamesh
- 700 BC

Aristotle (384 BC – 322 BC): A Greek philosopher, student of Plato and teacher of Alexander the Great. Aristotle is generally regarded as one of the most influential ancient thinkers in a number of philosophical fields, including: physics, metaphysics, poetry, theater, music, logic, rhetoric, politics, government, ethics, biology and zoology.

Code of Hammurabi created 1760 BC: Is one of the first law codes in history, for ancient Babylon (modern day Iraq). Created by the sixth Babylonian king, Hammurabi (1795BC-1750 BC), the first king of Babylon.

Code of Manu (200BC): Also known as Manusmrti, is generally regarded as the most authoritative and important of Sanskrit legal texts, the Dharmaśāstra textual tradition of Hinduism.

Confucius (551 BC – 479 BC): An influential Chinese thinker, educator and social philosopher, whose teachings and philosophy deeply influenced Chinese, Korean, Japanese, Taiwanese and Vietnamese thought and life. The teachings of Confucius have been amalgamated into a systemized philosophy called Confucianism.

Doctrine of Ma'at (3000 BC - 1240 BC): Found on the Papyrus of Ani, also known as the Book of the Dead. Ma'at is an ancient Egyptian declarations and spells, usually found on hieroglyphs, to assist the dead in the afterlife.

Homer (800 BC (approximate)): An ancient Greek poet, and allegedly the author of the *Iliad* and the *Odyssey* (the oldest existing work of Greek literature).

Horace (65BC – 8 BC): Officially known as Quintus Horatius Flaccus, is a Roman/Latin lyric poet. Along with Ovid and Virgil, he is considered one of the three canonic poets of Latin literature.

Ovid (43 BC – 17AD):   Officially known as Publius Ovidius Naso, a Roman/Latin poet who wrote about love, seduction, and mythological transformation. Along with Horace and Virgil, he is considered one of the three canonic poets of Latin literature.

Plato (428 BC – 348 BC): A Greek philosopher, and one of the most important writers in the Western Literary tradition.   Plato founded the Academy in Athens, the first institute of higher learned in Western society.

Pilibus Syrus (1ˢᵗ Century BC) : An Assyrian, became a slave in Italy, where he was ultimately freed and educated by his master, due to his intellect and aptitude. Pilibus wrote a series of "maxims," which were singe sentence adages, that flourished during his time.

Virgil (700 BC – 19 BC): Officially known as Publius Vergilius Maro, was a classical Roman poet, known primarily for what is now Rome's national epic, *Aeneid*. Along with Ovid and Horace, he is considered one of the three canonic poets of Latin literature.

About the author....

James Schaffer is a philosopher from San Diego State University. James currently lives in San Francisco, CA.

www.ingramcontent.com/pod-product-compliance
Lightning Source LLC
Chambersburg PA
CBHW020253290526
45784CB00003B/1227